See the Dragons
A Collection of Zen Haiku

poems by

E.B. Littlehill

Finishing Line Press
Georgetown, Kentucky

*In memory of my mother,
Mildred (Millie) Kleinberg*

See the Dragons
A Collection of Zen Haiku

Copyright © 2017 by E.B. Littlehill
ISBN 978-1-63534-285-7 First Edition
All rights reserved under International and Pan-American Copyright Conventions.
No part of this book may be reproduced in any manner whatsoever without written permission from the publisher, except in the case of brief quotations embodied in critical articles and reviews.

Publisher: Leah Maines

Editor: Christen Kincaid

Cover Art: E.B. Littlehill

Author Photo: Sean Jamar, seanjamar.com

Cover Design: Elizabeth Maines McCleavy

Printed in the USA on acid-free paper.
Order online: www.finishinglinepress.com
also available on amazon.com

Author inquiries and mail orders:
Finishing Line Press
P. O. Box 1626
Georgetown, Kentucky 40324
U. S. A.

For Deepak Chopra, who awakened my desire,
Sean Jamar Rhinehart, who lit the passion of my desire
&
Yukari Nagasawa, who nourished my desire

With Gratitude

Gratitude to the following who directly, or indirectly, brought this book to fruition: Rose Blessing, Carl Selinger & The Write Group, Anna McClean, reg e gaines, Donna Rockwell, John Baralle, Milton Kleinberg, Joshua Bedrosian, the Old Gang in Exile, Yung Pueblo, Eckhart Tolle, Oprah Winfrey, the Buddha, and Unbounded Consciousness.

Introduction

Dragons
I see the dragons
Envy Shame Fear Ego Hate
Vanish in the light

See the Dragons ~ A Collection of Zen Haiku began life in 2014 on my Tumblr blog, *Smoke Signals from the Hill*. The first Zen Haiku that tumbled into my awareness was about blueberry pie:

Blueberry Pie
Summer is over
And I baked only two pies
Farewell, blueberries

The summer of 2014 was a tough year for blueberries and the people who love to eat them. The price for a pint of the purple pleasures hovered at $2.50—a stark contrast to the summer before when prices fell as low as 89 cents. I baked about 11 pies back then.

What I lacked in blueberry pie creations was mitigated by a flood of Zen Haiku that poured out from a place of abundance I had only experienced once before, many years ago, when I wrote a manuscript of dub poetry.

Writing and anxiety always seem to be intertwined. Why I chose journalism, then later, marketing communications as careers from which to make a living is beyond me. My search for the perfect words that would lure a reader into a story (without resorting to cliché or fakery) was like wandering alone, at night, through a forest of fear. Oftentimes, I'd stuff down self-doubt with something to eat. When the deadline loomed for a feature story I was writing for a monthly magazine, I'd find fortification at the David's Cookies shop near my office in the Daily News building on East 42nd Street in Manhattan. With a half-pound bag of chocolate chip and oatmeal raisin close by on my desk, I was able to summon enough confidence to bang out the copy. Every month I'd lose, then gain back again, the same five or six pounds.

So what happened in 2014 when I wrote as many as 10 poems a day without gaining a pound of panic-weight? Two experiences converged.

First, I had nearly one solid year of a daily meditation practice under my belt. In the silence of sitting, I was finding my voice. Second, I started a romance with a man whose touch unleashed the poetry-power hiding inside something as mundane as a blueberry pie.

Smoke Signals From the Hill morphed into a chronicle of our romance within the context of my expanding awareness through meditation. Zen Haiku about love—romantic, unrequited and spiritual—filled my blog. I never had to sit, scratching my head, staring at a blank computer screen, searching for something to write about. I went with the flow wherever it took me.

And it took me to here. To this book you hold in your hands.

The Zen Haiku are divided into three sections: Romantic Love, Unrequited Love and Spiritual Love.

Thank you for reading and *namasté*.

Romantic Love

Eyelids

Behind my eyelids
In silent meditation
Is your face, your soul

Dream

I just want to dream
To float in the bliss of you
And do nothing else

Kiss

You're always in me
Happiness that lay dormant
Your kiss awakened

Muse

My heart wants to write
Bathe in the morning light's bliss
In the arms of love

United

You are inside me
I feel your spirit essence
Twin flames united

Black Balloon

My lips crave your lips
My black balloon addiction
Heroin of lust

Blaze

Your soul consumes me
Your spirit enters my own
Your touch is a blaze

Soul Connection

Do you feel it too?
Our soul connection of bliss
Weightless in freedom

Dreams of Desire

We get high, then drift
Into dreams of desire
My soul's protector

Remnants

I inhale remnants
Vestiges of our union
I relive the night

Golden Hour

My golden hour
A time when words of love flow
Creating our bliss

Insecurity

I often wonder
What it is you see in me
Will it sustain us?

Imagining

Imagining you
Feeling you deep within me
My soul surrenders

Duality

When I am with you
Duality disappears
I am bathed in light

Daydream

I daydream, blissful
While meditating on smiles
Intimate moments

Fantasy Photos

Fantasy photos
Captured in a web of love
Divine ecstasy

Awake

You awake in me
What I long to awaken
In your dream of me

Knowing

I feel your sweet hands
Your gentle knowing of me
Pure love awakens

Aura

Longing for your touch
Alone in my morning bed
I feel your aura

Invade

I invade your dreams
A subtle awakening
Second chakra bliss

Seed

Your essence was seed
To my creative spirit
Fertile with longing

Distraction

You, a distraction
From what I am meant to be
You are paradise

LL&B

I feel your spirit
You fill my second chakra
With love, light and bliss

Good Morning Texts

Your good morning texts
Electronic love letters
Ignite my longing

Business Casual

Incense and blue dream
Permeates business casual
Passion before work

Reconnecting

Your spirit fades out
Our connection is broken
Now, reconnecting

Dove Wings

I feel our two souls
Gentle exploring hopeful
Dancing on dove wings

Love Songs

Summertime tree frogs
I surrender my spirit
Into your love songs

Helium Rapture

We are the balloon
A black balloon filled with lust
Helium rapture

Spirit of Love

Your face before me
Your arms envelop my soul
Your spirit of love

Unrequited Love

Heroin Kiss

If someone warned me
Your kisses were heroin
I'd shoot them up still

Heartbeat

You were my heartbeat
Letting me know I was love
Now, I hear silence

Junk Food

My jeans feel so tight
Strangling the junk food I ate
Yet, I'm still empty

Waterfall

I grasp for your love
Forgetting it was sweeter
When it flowed to me

Advice

"Don't lie to yourself"
A friend's advice stings my heart
Stabbing at my truth

Shattered

I break my own heart
Shatter my mind's illusions
Mourn the death of hope

Desire

Desire's flame burns
Hot, fast with my lust for you
Then ashes of trust

Silence

Your silence stabs me
Bleeding out my love for you
Into creation

Fear

Fear is in my mind
Scenarios of anger
Alone in my bed

Goddess

Your goddess beckons
And it is not my presence
That brings you to love

Tree Frogs

Little tree frog friends
Vanish in the autumn chill
Like my love's embrace

Ashes

I opened my heart
To the flames of desire
Then there were ashes

Regrets

Longing for your kiss
A buzz, intoxication
Hangover regrets

Sit In My lap

"Come, sit in my lap."
Tender soul eyes beckon me
I'll be fooled again

Questions

I waste my own time
Was any of your love real?
A tiny sliver?

Teardrops

Every word stabs me
As I write of jealous rage
Teardrops fill my wounds

Yours

Miss your hands on me
Sliding up my leg, my hip
Knowing me as yours

Delusion

Two connected souls
Was it just self-delusion?
Mist on the mountains

Tears

My soul misses you
My spirit craves your embrace
Tears propel my words

Rust

Cold rust coats my lock
Separates me from my muse
My soul cries its words

Shattered Dreams

I taste your kisses
In my shattered dreams of lust
My wish won't come true

Not Me

Did you find kindness?
Did you open your hard heart?
To someone, not me

Shackles

In shackles I lay
Trapped in a cell of longing
I'm your prisoner

Silence

Conflicts unspoken
We sit in awkward silence
What happened to us?

Hands

My body misses
The feel of your hands on it
You possess my heart

Lies

Were all of your words
Every soulful kiss and touch
Lies you told to me?

Surrender

Wasn't I enough?
Didn't I love your body?
Surrender my soul?

Songbirds

Faintly in the wind
Whispers of loss and longing
Songbirds sing regret

Woman

I am a woman
Who only wanted to love
Your spirit, your soul

Happiness

There is lonely space
Where his love once filled my soul
Yet, he is happy

Spiritual Love

Freedom

When I became light
The door to my cage opened
Freedom from your spell

Let Go

Because I love you
I surrender, let you go
Into consciousness

Fingertips

Sunbeams heat my thigh
As your caresses once did
Fingertips of light

Never

My heart drinks freedom
Light, cosmic intelligence
It was never you

Creation

I reveal my soul
The light of my spirit flows
Into creation

Awareness

I am awareness
Secrets of the universe
Are all inside me

Reality

I'll always love you
You don't have to love me back
That's reality

Grace

Gratitude gives light
Being in a state of grace
My awareness grows

Now

Being in the now
Frees my mind from fearful thoughts
I feel who I am

Being

Relax into this:
Being light from nothingness
Being in pure love

Surrender

Set my intention
Letting the cosmic dance flow
Surrender to fate

Same Same

What will today bring?
Will it be happy or sad?
It's all the same thing

Perfection

Drifting on my thoughts
Bathing in perfection, bliss
Connected to all

Stars

Beyond my ego
Into cosmic connection
With the stars of grace

Truest Light

My truest light shines
When I am still and listen
To the voice within

Thief

The thief of my soul
It wasn't you after all
But ego and pride

Rejection

It's not rejection
It's cosmic redirection
To the light within

Compassion

Soul to soul oneness
Connecting in compassion
Free from blame and shame

Destiny

My destiny calls
To be present in the now
To follow my bliss

Journey

The journey to self
Twisting in upon itself
Begins at the end

Dreamcatcher

Fragile dream catcher
Frayed from fighting my nightmares
You guide me to now

Happy

My soul feels happy
I let go of attachment
My love is my own

Dissolving

It was never you
Sweet, deluded dreams dissolve
Into my wholeness

Letting Go

Do you feel my heart?
My blood flows with forgiveness
You, me, letting go

Peace

I live in the now
Observer of my own life
Peace envelops me

Existence

Travel in darkness
Swim through muddy waters
Into existence

Diving

Diving into bliss
Diving into my oneness
I meet my true self

Secret

Meet me in the now
I am the present moment
I am the secret

The Key

I bang at the door
Hoping to be let back in
The key is within

Radiance

My elusive love
Shimmers in the distant space
Between truth and mist

E.B. Littlehill is a former journalist and marketing communications writer. After being downsized from her corporate communications job during the Great Recession (she is still trying to figure out what was so great about it) she started a new career as a freelance event photographer. In 2014, she began a Tumblr blog of poetry and photographs called *Smoke Signals from the Hill*. She recently reached over 1,000 followers. All but a handful are complete strangers.

Her zen haiku, "Awareness," won Special Category Award: Haiku in the Spirit First 2016 Meditation Poetry Contest. HaikUniverse published her zen haiku "Time," and her poem, "Instagram Photos" was chosen for inclusion in the *Montclair Write Group Sampler 2016*.

www.ingramcontent.com/pod-product-compliance
Lightning Source LLC
LaVergne TN
LVHW041508070426
835507LV00012B/1412